FIXING *Our* EYES
A Guidebook for a TV-Free Week

Fixing Our Eyes

A Guidebook
for a TV-Free
Week

Our Eyes

KEVIN C. LEE

Tyndale House Publishers, Inc.
Wheaton, Illinois

Visit Tyndale's exciting Web site at www.tyndale.com

For more information on *Fixing Our Eyes* please visit www.fixingoureyes.org
or E-mail us at mail@fixingoureyes.org

Fixing Our Eyes: A Guidebook for a TV-Free Week

Edited by Jeremy P. Taylor

Designed by Kelly Bennema

ISBN 0-8423-5415-8

Printed in the United States of America

05 04 03 02 01
8   7   6   5   4   3   2   1

All proceeds from the sale of this book will be donated to foreign missions.

*For persons around the world who possess so
little, suffer so greatly, and cry out for a Savior.
May we devote ourselves more fully to bringing the
gospel of Jesus Christ to them.*

*"Has not God chosen those who are poor in the
eyes of the world to be rich in faith and to inherit
the kingdom he promised those who love him?"*

James 2:5

Let us fix our eyes on Jesus, the author and perfecter of our faith, who for the joy set before him endured the cross, scorning its shame, and sat down at the right hand of the throne of God.

Hebrews 12:2

Contents

TV-Free Week Pledge Page

I, _____ , hereby agree to
the following TV-Free Week pledge:

1. I agree to try a "life free from TV" for one entire
   week. This promise includes abstaining from movies,
   video games, and noneducational computer use.

2. I agree to complete one chapter in this *Fixing Our
   Eyes* guidebook each day during my TV-free week.

3. I agree to make productive use of the time I normally
   devote to television watching, keeping a positive
   attitude and sense of humor.

4. I agree to take prompt action on any changes the
   Lord directs me to make in my television viewing
   habits.[1]

Signed _____

   Date _____

Introduction

Fixing Our Eyes is a devotional guidebook designed to help Christians initiate lifelong changes in their television viewing habits during a TV-free week. There are seven guidebook sessions—one for each day of your "fast" from television.

Some twenty-five years ago, author Marie Winn organized the first weeklong "TV Turnoff" in Denver, Colorado.[2] Since that time, thousands of churches, schools, and communities have participated in seven-day periods without TV. This year, an estimated seven million persons will participate. So take heart! You won't be alone in your TV-free experiment. Enjoy it!

Four Steps to Success

Do you recall the warning "Don't try this at home"? Well, forget it this week, because you're going to jump into this adventure with both feet! Here's the four-step plan for a successful TV-free week:

1. *Sign* the TV-Free Week Pledge Page in the front of the book.
2. *Turn off* all of your television sets completely for the week.
3. *Complete* one guidebook chapter each day.
4. *Act* on any changes you decide to make with regard to TV watching in your home.

Suggestions

Get the Whole Family Involved

Promote the idea to your whole family. Explain to your kids that it is an important "experiment." Kids also may respond to the promise of a reward at week's end.[3]

Plan Ahead

Schedule some healthy activities during your TV-free week: a trip to the library, a dinner with friends, a family game night, a hiking/biking trip, a visit to a planetarium, a concert, a ball game. (See Appendix A for more ideas!)

Hide Your TVs . . .

Move the television sets out of your living room and bedrooms. Don't underestimate the magnetic power of TV sets: they will *stare* at you every time you enter a room, urging you to "just see what's on." (Seriously!) Lock them away in the garage or guest room. If a TV is too big to move, turn it around, unplug it, and drape an afghan over it. (Be sure to coordinate this with the decorator of the house.)

. . . and Remotes

Don't forget to hide the remotes! Stuff them in your sock drawer, or mail them to Aunt Edna. There! You're on your way!

Let the Book Be "The Heavy"

If spouse or kids grumble, say, "The *book* says we have to." Remind them that going without TV for a week has never proved fatal, and that millions are trying it.

If You're Having a Tough Time without TV . . .

That may not be all bad. Marie Winn explains: "Often those families that have the hardest time during their TV-Turnoff have the easiest time taking action afterward. The need for better television control becomes overwhelmingly clear to them as they suffer withdrawal pangs during the 'cold turkey' period, and they begin to see that nothing short of extreme measures will allow them to accomplish this control."[4]

A Joyful Heart Is Good Medicine

Proverbs 17:22 reminds us that a healthy sense of humor and a godly sense of purpose will help make your TV-free week a positive contribution to your walk with the Lord.

Keep a Journal

You may want to write down some of your thoughts during your TV-free week while they are fresh in your mind. You can use a notepad, typewriter, or computer. Questions to respond to might include:

• How has television viewing influenced my Christian life?
• How does life without television affect my daily activities?
• How do I feel about missing programs that I am used to watching?
• *Why* have I watched the programs I have watched?
• How can I best use my time?

Okay, you're ready to go! Remember to work through one chapter of this book each day of your TV-free week: chapter 1 on day one, chapter 2 on day two, etc. Try some of the alternative activities listed in Appendix A. Enjoy your experience! This could be your first step toward a healthier, happier life with less television. If you experience some difficulty sticking to your commitment, don't give up. If you stumble, pick yourself up and get back in there! Good luck, and may God bless you as you embark upon your TV-free week!

CHAPTER ONE

Fixing Our Eyes

O Jesus, nothing may I see, nothing desire,
or seek, but thee.
—John Wesley[1]

In a small Appalachian town, a tall, bronze statue of John Wesley quietly watches over a college campus that bears his name. People climb on him as they pose for photos, tape posters on him, and generally treat his likeness with indifference.

Mindful of the devotion and insight of this great eighteenth-century preacher, sometimes I wonder what sort of reaction the real Wesley would have to contemporary America. Were he to visit you for a day, what would he say?

He might well marvel at modern transportation—cars, trucks, and planes. He'd be duly impressed with your telephone, your stove, your refrigerator. But what about your television? How would you explain *that* to him?

"It's a remarkable communication device," you might tell him, "bringing moving pictures to your home from around the world—color pictures accompanied by voices and music."

"Amazing!" he says. "People in my day only dreamed of such things."

You explain that it offers information and entertainment

paid for by advertisers. "It's very popular—nearly every home has at least one TV. In fact, the typical American household spends more than seven hours a day watching it."

"Seven hours a day!" Wesley responds. "That's remarkable! What kind of pictures do people spend half of their waking hours watching? Symphonies? Orators?"

"Not usually," you say. "Let's see, people watch sporting events, comedy skits, and drama shows . . ."

"Hmmm . . . can we watch one now?" he asks.

"Uh . . . ," you say hesitantly. "A lot of the dramas have murders and adultery—but they're just acting, you understand. And, uh, some of the comedies have some mighty strong language and bad situations."

"That's awful," Wesley concludes. "Surely Christians like yourself have spoken out against this frightful activity."

"Well . . . not exactly," you say.

Hard to Explain

It is not difficult to imagine the shock that a devoted Christian from the past such as John Wesley would have if he viewed just a few hours of the parade of violence and promiscuity on modern television. True, Wesley lived in an era that was much different from ours. But there is little question that there are enough bad shows broadcast every night of the week to make godly people throughout history mourn.

However, those who have gone before us might be even more shocked to discover the reaction of Christians to this incredible phenomenon of modern culture. Not only have many believers done very little about the horrible content of today's television programs, some of them devote more of their time to television watching than to any other single activity besides sleep and work!

Imagine trying to describe a sitcom or a police show to one of Christ's disciples—and explain *why* God's people today are watching them day after day after day. Is our focus in the wrong place? What in the world has happened to today's Christians? Indeed something *is* broken. We need to fix our eyes . . . and our hearts.

Look Straight Ahead

Baseball players are told "keep your eye on the ball" when batting and fielding. Toddlers often are reminded to "watch where you're going" when learning to walk. The fact is that our visual focus of attention is crucial to our performance and safety. The objects upon which we focus our eyes have significant power to control our path of travel. This is true in both the physical and the spiritual realms.

"Let your eyes look straight ahead," the Bible tells us. "Fix your gaze directly before you. Make level paths for your feet and take only ways that are firm" (Proverbs 4:25-26).

The magnetic draw of what we look at is so strong, in fact, that it often causes accidents. Fighter pilots fall prey to "target fixation" when they focus so intently on their targets that they fly right into the ground. Drivers and bicyclists suffer similar accidents when they look too long at objects on the side of the road.

One bicycling magazine counseled its readers, "Have you ever seen a big boulder in the middle of the trail that you wanted to avoid—and then run right into it? There's a simple reason: The bike tends to go where you look. . . . The solution is to focus ahead on the good line that cuts through the clutter."[2] That's great advice for the Christian, too! Jesus even tells us to travel on his "narrow" road (Matthew 7:14).

Where to Look

Want to know where to look physically and spiritually? The Bible gives clear directions. God's Word warns us to *avoid* looking at certain things and encourages us to *focus* on others.

Jesus said, "No one who puts his hand to the plow and looks back is fit for service in the kingdom of God" (Luke 9:62). Lot's wife, longing to return to Sodom, ignored a similar warning from God and forfeited her life (Luke 17:32-33). David's sin with Bathsheba started with a forbidden look (2 Samuel 11:2). Our eyes need to be directed by God, not by our sinful desires.

The Lord gives his people the privilege of seeing things that stir their souls. As part of a short-term mission team to the former Soviet Union a few years ago, I watched people of all ages *rush* into small-town auditoriums to hear the gospel. Those who attended our evangelistic services hung on every translated word and song we shared. At the end they *surged* forward to receive Bibles in their language.

"I tell you, *open your eyes* and *look* at the fields!" Christ exhorts us. "They are ripe for harvest" (John 4:35, emphasis added). Indeed, we should focus our eyes and hearts on the wonderful people the Lord has made all around the world— many so ready for the gospel.

One noteworthy couple—with their spiritual eyes on the lost—returned from a missions trip to Haiti determined to change. They pared down their possessions and started a missions-minded Sunday school class. They stopped their cable-TV subscription and sent that thirty dollars a month to support the Great Commission. [3]

For spiritual clarity, we are encouraged to "fix our eyes on Jesus, the author and perfecter of our faith" (Hebrews 12:2). John the Baptist gave a similar command when he proclaimed, "Look, the Lamb of God, who takes away the sin of the world!" (John 1:29). It is exciting to think that one day we shall see the full glory of Christ, as Christ himself said in John 17:24: "Father, I want those you have given me to be with me where I am, and to see my glory."

Questions

1. Read the following Scriptures. For each set, explain what kinds of things God would have us refrain from looking at with our physical and/or spiritual eyes.

   Psalm 101:3; Psalm 119:37

   Genesis 9:22-23; Habakkuk 2:15

Genesis 19:17, 26; Luke 17:30-33

Job 31:1; Matthew 5:28; 2 Peter 2:14

2. For each of the following Scriptures, explain what God would have us look at spiritually and/or physically.

2 Corinthians 4:18

Psalm 19:8, Psalm 119:18

John 4:35

Psalm 123:1-2, Hebrews 12:1-2

3. Read Matthew 6:22-23. Does the way we use our eyes affect our physical and spiritual condition? Explain.

4. Sometimes our ability to see is part of God's blessing; at other times it is a method of retribution. Read the following verses. For each one, describe the actions of people and of God.

Acts 9:1-9

Genesis 19:1-11

1 John 2:10-11

Ephesians 1:18-19

Psalm 135:15-18

Isaiah 33:15-17

Zephaniah 1:17

For Additional Reading

- Scriptures: Psalm 25:15; Psalm 141:8
- Look up the following terms in a Bible concordance, dictionary, or reference book: eye/eyes; focus; fix (your eyes upon . . .); gaze; look; watch.

CHAPTER TWO

Watch Your Time

> *What I mean, brothers, is that the time is*
> *short. . . . For this world in its present form*
> *is passing away.*
> —1 Corinthians 7:29, 31

Answering a knock at your door, you are greeted by an energetic representative for a volunteer organization. "Hi, my name is Samantha!" she exclaims. "I'm with Project Playground, and we're asking people in your community to give three hours a day, seven days a week to help develop recreation programs for area kids."

"Oh, my," you say with a laugh. "I appreciate your enthusiasm, and that's a fine cause. But there is no way in the world I could volunteer that much time! I don't think you'll find anyone *that* devoted. Good luck."

Closing the door, you begin to wonder who could possibly find the time—in addition to work, family, and church—to give up three hours every waking day. Wait a minute! It might be *you*. Three hours a day is precisely the type of time commitment many Christians have made to watching TV! In fact, some devote almost *twice* that much time to the tube.

Abundant Life
Christ desires for us to "live life to the full" (John 10:10). What a blessing! And when we are encouraged by a

televised sermon or have our day brightened by a whole-some comedy, television can be part of it! But what about the rest of your TV time?

Consider a typical evening of ho-hum television, spanning from dinnertime to lights out. Afterward someone asks, "So, did you enjoy your evening of TV?"

Enjoy it? An evening of plain old TV? That seems like an odd question. "It was just TV, you know."

When you think about it, television watching is seldom a remarkable experience. It's probably not what Jesus had in mind when he spoke about the "full" life. It's just TV, you know.

Who else, honestly, is going to benefit from your TV watching? Nobody at all, most of the time! And it may seldom be of any lasting value to *you*, the viewer. Television watching can be an enormously selfish and unsatisfying activity, an unnecessary waste of the precious time you have been given.

Pizza, Anybody?

Pizza, many would say, is a staple of the American diet. It's the rare soul who will turn down a slice of that delicious dinnertime treat. I, for one, love those cheesy pies—thin crust or thick, one topping or ten. Just let me at 'em! However, at times I've given in to the urge for "just one more slice." Ugh! Then even the best pizza leaves me stranded on the corner of the sofa while I "digest." The blessing of eating can be overwhelmed by the agony of gluttony.

Human beings should not *gorge* themselves on anything. Even the healthiest foods become unhealthy if we stuff ourselves sick with them. The same principle applies to what we subject our eyes and minds to. How can we followers of Christ justify three or four—or *seven or more*—hours of television *every single day?* No matter what measure you use, that's excessive visual gluttony! And little of television's regular fare qualifies as health food for the mind.

Do we spend that much time reading God's Word? Are we that caught up on our prayer concerns? Have we spent so much quality time with our families and friends that we can veg out on videos or feed on football?

Your Time: Spent or Squandered?

Author Michael Medved notes, "By the age of six, the average American child has spent more hours watching the tube than he will spend speaking to his father in his lifetime."[1]

Does God care how we spend our time? Does it matter to the Lord if you squander an evening lounging in the recliner, remote in hand, while your teenager agonizes alone in her room over a difficult decision? Does it hurt God if you choose to watch a bad movie or a second-rate ball game on Saturday when the day's Bible-study lesson sits untouched on your bedside table?

What about when family members try to "contact you" while you are watching the tube: "Hey, Mom, may I talk with you? Mom? Mom!" But they lose the competition for your attention. "Just a minute!" you say impatiently. "I'm trying to watch this." You tell your spouse or child, "I'll take care of that when the TV program is over."

Do you regularly choose TV over family? Consider how you might finish this statement: I really have trouble finding time to:

1. spend time with my kids.
2. volunteer for a task at church.
3. take care of something around the house.
4. join my spouse for a long-overdue date.
5. do any of the above.

Tube Time

How many hours do *you* spend watching television? Better think carefully and add them all up; many people underestimate. Let's say you spend 3.5 hours daily, significantly less than the national average. That's 24.5 hours a week. At that rate, you're devoting one entire day out of every single *week* to television!

Annually, at 24.5 hours a week, you're burning up 1,274 hours. That's 53 full, round-the-clock days of TV watching every year—almost 2 complete months out of every 12 entirely given over to television! You can kiss January and July goodbye; they were spent in front of the TV. Think about it. These are real hours and days and years for which the Lord has given you strength and breath.

At 24.5 hours a week, how much of your life will you surrender to TV? If you begin watching at age 3 and end at age 73, you will have 89,180 complete hours of television viewing on your account. That's 3,716 days, or 124 months . . . or *10 years!* One *decade* of your life! And if you're a seven-hour-a-day TV junkie, it's *two* decades.

Hebrews 9:27 tells us that "man is destined to die once, and after that to face judgment." Picture yourself at the end of your time on earth, standing in front of the Lord, trying to justify devoting 10 or 20 full years, night and day, to watching television. Pinch yourself. These are not hypothetical hours expanded by some alarmist. These are the years of *your* life! Imagine trying to explain why you chose to watch tens of thousands of murders, acts of adultery, and curses on the screen instead of immersing yourself in healthy activities.

Christians who continue to waste God's precious time watching unhealthy images on television—especially during the most productive years of their lives—will suffer the consequences, period. God doesn't lie. He is not going to say, "Well done, good and faithful servant" to those who haven't been good or faithful. That would be a mockery to those who have.

The portions of our lives surrendered to regrettable TV watching will never be returned. They are gone. Hours are not like coupons that can be redeemed later for more time with children or service for the Lord. Squandering your time is a costly mistake.

Good vs. Best

"Wait a minute," you may say. "I don't watch the *bad* shows. I watch pretty good stuff, really—sports, nature programs, news."

As Christians we have been challenged to *prioritize* our time investments. God urges us to be "very careful" how we live, making the most of our time on this earth "because the days are evil" (Ephesians 5:15-16). Jesus compels us to get to work, for "night is coming when no one can work" (John 9:4). Watching *Jeopardy* won't help those whose eternal lives are in *real* jeopardy.

Sometimes our choices as Christians are good vs. best. Are we devoting time to God and family, recreation and fellowship—or entertainment and amusement? Ask yourself, *What is the best thing I could be doing this day, this month?* Ask God, *What is your will for me this afternoon, this week?* We are to follow God's Word as it lights our path (Psalm 119:105), not the eerie blue glow of the television. We are to be "led by the Spirit" (Romans 8:14). "So I say, live by the Spirit, and you will not gratify the desires of the sinful nature" (Galatians 5:16).

If we are not "very careful"—as Ephesians 5:15 says—relatively good things can crowd out the best. TV watching is rarely the *best* way you could be investing your life for God.

Can you name a specific program that should rightly take precedence over quiet time with God? Will you choose *Good Morning America* over a godly morning in prayer? Should we spend more time daily with television than we do with our Bibles? What if we timed ourselves? How much time do we set aside daily for prayer, worship, and reading the Bible and Christian books compared with the amount of time we devote to the tube? You can say resolutely, "I missed my quiet time this morning, so no TV for me until I meet with the Lord." This need not be an exercise in legalism, driven only by duty, but one of devotion, motivated by love.

"Train yourself to be godly," the apostle Paul compels us (1 Timothy 4:7). In Acts, the early Christians "devoted themselves" to Bible teaching, prayer, and Christian gatherings (Acts 2:42). We, too, should not "merely listen to the word," but "do what it says" (James 1:22).

It's Eye Catching

Today, Christians squander many free evenings with their eyes glued to the TV set, remote in hand, churning through the channels in search of something to watch. It's cheaper than cigarettes; it's more convenient than beer. For many people, TV is just plain addictive, like alcohol or tobacco.

According to Rutgers University psychologist Robert Kubey, persons who exhibit *four* or more dependency symptoms are clinically diagnosed with "substance abuse." Kubey notes that heavy TV viewers typically display as many as *six* symptoms of dependency:

1. Feeling loss of control while viewing
2. Indiscriminate viewing
3. Using television as a sedative
4. Feeling angry with oneself for watching too much
5. Inability to stop watching
6. Feeling miserable when kept from watching[2]

When a person gets lung cancer after years of cigarette smoking, whose fault is it? When a person gets cirrhosis of the liver after years of drinking, who's to blame? You may have even heard their denials: "Oh, I don't think anything bad is going to happen to *me*. I feel fine."

What about TV dependency? When a viewer habitually watches disgusting television programs—and is subsequently haunted by bawdy and violent images—whose fault is it?

> [O]ur compulsive involvement with the tube often keeps us from talking to each other, from doing things together, from working and learning and getting involved in community affairs. The hours we spend viewing prove to be curiously unfulfilling. . . . And yet we cannot seem to turn the set off, or even *not* turn it

on in the first place. Doesn't this sound like an addiction?[3]

Many kids grow up to smoke or drink because their parents did. Will the children of adults who are addicted to TV follow that destructive pattern? "I try to limit the kids' TV watching," one mother explained. "But Alfred, my husband, likes to watch quite a bit. Limiting the kids means he'd have to limit himself, and he doesn't really want to do that."[4]

Through the Holy Spirit, Christians are to nurture the fruit of self-control (Galatians 5:23). This includes television watching. You might ask yourself, *Do I own my television set, or does it own me?*

Desensitized

Regardless of whether you have "control" over your use of TV, the relentless repetition of messages will inevitably affect your mind. It's like the man who argues that a little alcohol won't perceptibly alter his judgment because he can "hold his liquor." In other words, he has consumed enough of the stuff that it no longer has the impact on him it first did. Along the way, however, an enormous number of living cells in his brain and internal organs have been annihilated. Also, on those occasions when he seeks a little "buzz" from the alcohol, he must consume a higher quantity of drink.

Ironically, many Christians make the same argument regarding television programming and video rentals. They don't let their kids watch R-rated material, of course, but *they've* seen so much of this sort of thing before that it no longer bothers them. Like an alcoholic or a nicotine addict, they have become desensitized to everything but the "strong stuff." To satisfy this desire for a stronger product, today's television and videos feature sin in shocking excess—the crudest innuendoes, the most offensive insults, the boldest adultery, the most shocking horror and gruesome violence, the most abrasive, the silliest, the ugliest.

God's Word speaks of those who have "seared" their consciences (1 Timothy 4:2). Many Christians today are doing just that when they overload on suggestive sexual imagery, graphic violence, and crude language. It's difficult to respond to the call to "set [one's] mind on things above" when a veritable sea of sinful images is splashing around inside one's head (Colossians 3:2).

Few people would purposely place their hands on a hot burner and sear their flesh. The horrible pain is accompanied by lifelong scars. But what about our minds and hearts? Once, while flipping through channels with a remote, I ran across a murder scene on TV. From the few seconds I saw of it, the show seemed to involve mobsters. That brief murder scene was so brutal, so vicious, that it shocked me. I only saw it once, but in my mind it played over and over. The image was there, and the emotional message was there, too.

Yes, after viewing a disgusting show we can be "transformed by the renewing of our mind" (Romans 12:2), but it will take some time. We ought to stop and think about what is happening to our hearts, not just try to "shake it off" and jump right back into television's visual pigpen. There our minds will get soiled all over again.

Questions

1. Estimate the number of hours you have usually devoted to television watching in the past. Don't fudge; be honest! Review in your mind your standard routine for each day of the week, from waking up in the morning to going to sleep at night. Be sure to include morning, daytime, afternoon, and evening viewing habits.

   Fill in the blanks below with the number of hours for each day of the week. Total them. Then multiply by 52 (weeks) to derive your estimated annual hours. Then multiply that number by 70 (years) and use the result to derive your approximate lifetime hours.

Monday	_____
Tuesday	+_____
Wednesday	+_____
Thursday	+_____
Friday	+_____
Saturday	+_____
Sunday	+_____

   Weekly TOTAL = _____ hours

   _____ x 52= Annual TOTAL = _____ hours

   ____ x 70= Lifetime TOTAL = _____ hours

   (Divide by 24 =_____days; divide days by 30 =_____months (approx.); divide months by 12 =_____Years)

2. How do you feel about watching that much television?

3. Read Ephesians 5:15-16. How does God say that we should live?

How do you believe television watching fits in with this plan?

4. Read Luke 12:16-23. What was the rich man's perspective on how much time he had left on this earth?

How did he plan to spend his remaining time?

What did God think about all of this?

5. As Christians we have been challenged to *prioritize* our time investments: God, family, work, fellowship, recreation . . . entertainment? Read the following Scriptures, and explain how each relates to the challenge to use our time wisely.

2 Thessalonians 3:6-15

James 4:7-8

Proverbs 3:5-6

Proverbs 27:20

6. Read 1 Corinthians 6:12. How would you relate this passage to addictions?

7. Go for a walk. Or take a trip to the library and check out some good books or audio tapes. Or select another edifying activity from Appendix A and devote some time to it.

Optional Exercise

On a separate piece of paper, make a list of your regular time commitments: quiet time (Bible, prayer, godly books, etc.); family (eating together, talking, etc.); work/school; church/fellowship; sports/clubs (ball practice, Girl Scouts); exercise/recreation (walking, biking, swimming, racquetball); entertainment (TV, VCR, video games).

1. Prioritize your list, placing the most important at the top and working your way down.
2. Divide sixteen hours (the average number of hours spent awake each day) among the list, and give each a daily amount of what it *should* be. Example: Soccer Practice—2 hours (Tuesday, Thursday)
3. Now estimate how much time each item on your list is *really* given. Which items need to be given increased—or decreased—time?

CHAPTER THREE

Television: What a Character!

Television, at its best, has been greatly used to advance
God's purposes. Diligent believers have used television
programming and movies as tools to help communicate
edifying messages around the globe. Perhaps the most
remarkable example is the *Jesus* film—a 2-hour motion
picture on the life of Christ taken directly from the book
of Luke. As of the date of publication of this book, nearly
4 billion people in 233 countries have seen the *Jesus* film. In
167 of those nations, the film has been shown on television.
The film has been translated into more than 450 languages,
and there are over 24.3 million *Jesus* videos in circulation.[2]

Other ministries have brought evangelistic crusades to
large TV audiences and have borne lasting fruit. Christian
teachers have helped the Bible come alive with godly
teaching, video tours of the ancient world, and many other
edifying programs.

Dream Themes or Nightmares?

A great deal of secular television, however, provides a stark
contrast to gospel-centered programming. Dramas, comedies,

talk shows, and movies—sometimes even sports—often glamorize behaviors that damage lives. A number of entertainment shows feature some or all of the following five themes, crashing headlong through the clear warning signs in God's Word.

Theme #1: Go ahead, give in to ANGER

From the coach slamming down his clipboard to the hero punching out a villain, television is filled with dramatic portrayals of people losing their tempers.

In fits of rage, screen stars regularly scream at, beat up, chase, shoot, and kill their opponents. The Bible counsels us, "In your anger do not sin" (Psalm 4:4). Jesus told us to love and pray for our enemies. But when Clint Eastwood or Arnold Schwarzenegger are wronged, the message they send is "get mad and get even." And it's not just men! Today plenty of furious females, too, are cussing 'em out and blowing 'em away.

No doubt about it, angry characters make dramatic video—close-ups of shouting stars, fast-paced gun battles, and hair-raising car chases. Blood and bombs and bullets. Pretty exciting footage! And in the end, the bad guys get their due and the hero gets the glory.

But it's not like that in real life! Anger is one of the most destructive forces on the face of the earth. How many men and women have literally destroyed their lives, and the lives of their families, in just a single moment of rage? Angry words fuel countless divorces, crush the hearts of vulnerable children, and shipwreck churches. Angry actions can cause people to bruise, beat, and even kill family members. Anger can be dangerous, and it can send perpetrators to prison for decades.

Television watching doesn't literally cause people to "blow up," of course. But it would be foolish to say parents and kids can watch hour upon hour of violence with *no* effect at all. By age 18, the average American will have viewed more than 100,000 acts of violence, including nearly 10,000 murders.[3] Some "body bag" movies include a staggering amount of deadly aggression: one high-profile action film with a well-known cast included 264 murders.[4]

"Do not make friends with a hot-tempered man," Proverbs 22:24 warns. "Do not associate with one easily angered, or you may learn his ways and get yourself ensnared." Sad to say, there is every indication that many viewers have been "learning the ways" of the angry. Over three thousand studies show a strong correlation between the viewing of violent programming and physical and verbal aggression—particularly in boys.[5]

Theme #2: Go ahead, give in to LUST

There are people who want to keep our sex instinct inflamed in order to make money out of us. Because, of course, a man with an obsession is a man who has very little sales resistance.
—C. S. Lewis[6]

Men and women and teens on television today are following their sinful sexual urges in unprecedented fashion. Dramas, soaps, sitcoms, movies, talk shows, and news programs all buzz with explicit details of immoral relationships. It makes you wonder how much longer the Lord of heaven will wait before stepping in to say, "Enough!" Whether or not they view premarital sex and adultery as immoral, even the most callous viewers cannot deny that some TV programming has become saturated with sex.

Answering a question about the sexual differences between men and women, Dr. James Dobson notes:

> [M]en are primarily aroused by *visual* stimulation. They are turned on by female nudity and peek-a-boo glimpses of semi-nudity. Women . . . are much less visually oriented. . . . [H]e can become almost as excited over a photograph of an unknown nude model as he can in a face-to-face encounter with someone he loves. In essence, the sheer biological power of sexual desire in a male is largely focused on the physical body of an attractive female.[7]

Obviously this is no secret to the producers of contemporary TV and movies. A number of them have relentlessly devoted their talents to stirring up the sexual energies of male viewers. They routinely select strikingly attractive women for leading roles, dress them in provocative clothing, script them into tantalizing "adult situations" and zoom in the cameras. These scenes are highly alluring, extraordinarily tempting. No wonder we guys have such a struggle avoiding suggestive programs!

Christ said, "Anyone who looks at a woman lustfully has already committed adultery with her in his heart" (Matthew 5:28). How many men have been led into "heart adultery" night after night with the brazen women on the screen? Two or three women a night, two hundred or more nights a year—the numbers are enough to make Don Juan blush . . . and to make Jesus weep.

Some Christians stumble along in a stupor of guilt because deep in their hearts they *know* what they are doing, yet they continue to tune in to—and get turned on by— televised seductions. Ineffective and spiritually wounded, the TV adulterer passes the workday in a fog, mind filled with the haunting images of the night before—and the guilt of having given in.

Perhaps there are churches limping along, starved for leadership, while some of their Christian men sit spiritually sidelined, wasting away in the recliner, captivated by the TV temptress. Too many of these should-be leaders are spiritually sidelined, missing in action, their hearts devastated by a nightly barrage of seductively dressed starlets.

The Bible warns against giving in to the "charms" of such women, which lead only to death. "Do not lust in your heart after her beauty or let her captivate you with her eyes, for the prostitute reduces you to a loaf of bread, and the adulteress preys upon your very life" (Proverbs 6:25-26). "Why be captivated, my son, by an adulteress? Why embrace the bosom of another man's wife? For a man's ways are in full view of the Lord, and he examines all his paths" (Proverbs 5:20-21).

Theme #3: Go ahead, give in to COVETING

Long before uttering his first sentence, our oldest son would point longingly at the Golden Arches as we drove by and call out, "Fries!" But while parents groan, advertisers grin. They work very hard to make those kinds of encounters happen as often as possible on the roadway and in the supermarket.

Since many adults have developed brand loyalties, a

major target of the advertisers' arsenals are children and teens. Slick, sophisticated, seductive campaigns aim at turning your children into voracious, brand-loyal buyers. "Mom, I want a Happy Meal with *that* toy!"

The typical American child watches—are you ready for this?—20,000 television commercials *every year!* Advertisers are quite serious about your children, using sophisticated statistical analyses, focus groups, and test messages to sharpen sales pitches. They spend well over *half a billion dollars* annually on advertising aimed at kids. That's roughly the equivalent of a stack of $100 bills towering half a mile into the sky—over three times the height of the Sears Tower!

Jesus counseled that "a man's life does not consist in the abundance of his possessions" (Luke 12:15). Yet the relentless barrage of commercials on television urges viewers to covet, consume, and be happy—cars and toys, candy and clothes, and everything else you can imagine. Advertisers seek to captivate and motivate you, the consumer: "Hurry!" "Act now!" "No payments for twelve months!" "You can't afford to miss this sale!" "You *can* have it all, so just do it!"

Theme #4: Go ahead, give in to the TONGUE

Loose lips sink ships . . . and homes, and careers, and churches. But on television, folks say whatever they want to say, no matter how rude, sarcastic, or brutal. There are slanderous insults on the news, surly innuendoes on the sitcoms, shocking profanity on the action shows, and graphic sexual descriptions on the daytime talk shows.

The one who has the final word in eternity tells us, "Whoever would love life and see good days must keep

his tongue from evil and his lips from deceitful speech"
(1 Peter 3:10).

Theme #5: Go ahead, give in to LAZINESS

Just relax. Kick back on the sofa and just watch . . . and
watch . . . and watch. "Stay tuned!" "Coming up next . . ."
"We'll be right back!" "Don't go away!" "Here's a glimpse of
next week's episode—you won't want to miss this one!"
"Coming soon!" "Part IV."

We should hearken to God's advice: "Go to the ant, you
sluggard; consider its ways and be wise" (Proverbs 6:6).
Have you ever seen an ant with a remote? No way—there's
work to be done.

Anger, lust, covetousness, an uncontrolled tongue,
laziness—all are formidable challenges for today's Christian.
God's Word instructs us to flee temptation, resist the devil,
and exercise self-control through the Holy Spirit. What do
you do when you are tempted by what you see on TV? Do
you flee?

Television—A Different Sort of Vehicle

Imagine planning a trip to a distant city without considering
the transportation. "I'm going to get there any way you look
at it," you say. "So what difference does it make *how* I get
there?"

Actually, it makes all the difference in the world. Will
you go by plane, train, or car? motorcycle, bicycle, or
skateboard? Any of them may get you to your destination,
but you'll be a different person depending on *how* you get
there. Take a plane, and you'll arrive in a few hours, dressed
and ready for business. Ride a skateboard, and you might

travel for weeks in all kinds of weather. Travel experiences vary greatly according to vehicle.

The same is true with media—a magazine article about the city you plan to visit differs greatly from a radio show, and both differ greatly from a TV program. So, if we ask only whether the *message* is good, we're looking at the destination but ignoring the transportation. We're critiquing the lesson but ignoring the teacher—and television is a very different teacher from magazines, books, or radio.

Differences

How, then, does the character of this all-too-familiar medium differ from radio and print?

For one thing, content on TV is greatly influenced by its overwhelming need for pictures. Consider the action novel that becomes a TV movie. The author devoted several *pages* to the hero's escape plan in the book. But on the screen, it's trimmed to a few seconds. Indeed, a great deal is lost in the "translation" from print to video. Below are more unique qualities of television.

What's in a Name?

Television is so familiar—yet so mindless—that we give it nicknames. One can't be too serious about "the tube," "the idiot box," "the boob tube," or—as the British say—"the goggle box." But it has a dark side, too, so we call it "the one-eyed monster," "the plug-in drug," "the electronic babysitter," or "the Trojan horse."[8] Even its listless viewers are dubbed "couch potatoes" or "vidiots."

Eye-eye-eye

About every three seconds, television programs subject their audiences to visual "cuts." These rapid-fire edits shoot your attention to a different camera angle or location. A real-life equivalent might be closing your eyes, turning sharply, then quickly reopening your eyes—about twenty times every minute!

Our eyes are jerked around constantly by television. No wonder even the most inane programming is able to capture our attention—our eyes are being subjected to an electronic version of Chinese water torture.

TV Hangover

Have you ever walked in on someone deeply immersed in a TV show? There the person sits, eyes wide open, body slumped, mouth ajar, spaced out, mesmerized, hypnotized. After calling out the person's name a couple of times, you finally get a response of "Huh?"

A mesmerized viewer resembles the proverbial "deer in the headlights"—a clueless animal standing dead still in the middle of the highway as danger roars ever closer. All the person in such a situation can say is, "Wow, look at those lights!"

Wow, indeed. Something powerful is going on during those hours in front of the television. One author said she was concerned about television's effect on her children because of "the strange, trance-like way they sat and stared at the TV set, regardless of what they were watching."[9]

A friend of ours noticed an accompanying phenomenon with her two girls—they were always groggy and disagreeable following prolonged television viewing. She dubbed the condition "TV hangover."

The Bible exhorts us, "Wake up, O sleeper, rise from the dead, and Christ will shine on you" (Ephesians 5:14).

Front Room, Back Room

One communication scholar notes that humans wisely separate their lives into "front-room" behavior, suitable for the public, and "back-room" behavior, reserved only for oneself, one's family, and one's closest friends.[10] Like performers in the theater, we keep the curtain closed on the dressing and grooming backstage and share only public behavior onstage.

Yet television programmers routinely pull back the curtain on the private lives of human beings. We now live in a world where the media has deemed that nothing is sacred or even private. It's all on the screen. In their efforts to "push the envelope" they have even pointed their cameras into bathrooms and bedrooms.

In a world with video capabilities, perhaps some things are a "must-see," like a winning touchdown or baby's first step. But TV programs are now filled with many other things that our eyes should never, ever see on a video screen: private conflicts, gruesome murders, sexual encounters.

> Too many people in the evangelical community have come to justify watching on the screen various activities we wouldn't think of viewing in the flesh. Things that would embarrass us all if they were real, embarrass us not at all because they are only

simulated. . . .Yet to produce that love scene, two people who weren't married to each other pressed their undressed bodies to each other while millions of the rest of us watched and gave our sentimental assent. What we'd never do with our next-door neighbor we paid money to do with someone else's neighbor. [11]

The Bible says, "It is shameful even to mention what the disobedient do in secret" (Ephesians 5:12). And we are no less to blame for *watching* it—as entertainment, no less!

Just Watchin'

More than any other medium in contemporary society, television rushes in and eats up unstructured time. People habitually plop down on the sofa simply to "watch TV" without any particular program in mind . . . and find themselves still watching hours later! Just to "kill time," they'll watch whatever happens to be on—regardless of the content.

Questions

1. Read the following Scripture passages. Explain what each has to say about how we use our minds.

    Romans 12:2

Philippians 4:8

Colossians 3:2-3

Matthew 22:37

2. Read the following Scriptures. For each, describe what the Bible says about these common television themes:

a. Anger
Genesis 49:5-7

Psalm 37:8

James 1:19-20

b. Lust
Hosea 7:4

Proverbs 5:1-23

Matthew 5:27-30

c. Covetousness
1 Timothy 6:9-10

Acts 20:35

d. Tongue
Leviticus 24:10-16

James 3:2-8

Proverbs 10:19

e. Laziness
Proverbs 26:14-15

3. Read Matthew 7:24-27 and 1 Corinthians 3:10-15.
   How does God compare our lives to a construction project?

   How does God determine the quality of your building?

4. Find one or more ministries in Appendix B that interest you. If you like, contact them by phone or E-mail and request some free literature.

CHAPTER FOUR

Family

*These commandments that I give you today
are to be upon your hearts. Impress them
on your children.*

—Deuteronomy 6:6-7

"Enjoy your children!" a thoughtful pastor once counseled. My wife and I have taken this wise admonition to heart many times with our three energetic kids—sons aged eight and five and daughter aged three. One of their favorite prebedtime activities is the Indoor Motorcycle Race. Outstretched hands gripping invisible handlebars, mouths sputtering forth Harley noises, they race through the house. The meek in heart need not participate! They crash onto pillows, laughing uproariously. What a delight to watch!

Sure, our kids get loud at times, but they're not always roaring. Often they are wonderfully quiet. They love to build with blocks, play with toys, and draw pictures. They enjoy reading books and having us read to them. And they love to play outside—they ride bikes, dig in the sand, chase each other, and make up games.

God has equipped children with delightful imaginations that grow with wholesome input. Those wonderful young minds can transform furniture into fire engines and building blocks into skyscrapers. A box of Tinkertoys becomes a dinosaur, and the living room becomes a concert hall for their performances.

Sadly, excessive television viewing can stifle the creative process—kids aren't constructing pictures in their minds when they see images on the screen; they're not playing outside in God's beautiful earth or visiting friends when the TV camera takes them where *it* wants to go.

Parents metamorphosing into potatoes on the couch and kids sitting glassy-eyed on the floor are missing many of the creative joys of being a family. Tragically, the typical American household has at least two TVs and keeps them running seven hours or more every day. Forty percent of Americans watch the tube during dinner. More than half of the nation's children have a TV in their bedroom! One in four Americans falls asleep in front of the television at least three nights each week.[1]

Imagine how much more productive your family life could become if you just turned off the box. Instead of staring at the screen, try starting a wrestling match with your kids. Or spend time with your teenager. Read, build, exercise, explore, talk. The wonderful years you have with your family pass mighty quickly, so don't waste them!

Who's Watching the Kids?

> It is, of course, ironic that many parents avoid a TV turnoff out of fear that their children won't know what to do with themselves in the absence of television. It is television watching itself that has allowed them to grow up without learning how to be resourceful.[2]

Early in a child's life, often even before the very first birth-day, many Christian parents make a crucial, life-altering decision to use the TV set as an "electronic babysitter." Yes, they are tired and frustrated by the time demands placed on them by their hectic lives. But should we substitute television for the care of a parent or the development of a child's creativity?

It's tough for children—and parents too—to return to enriching activities once they've turned on the box. The whole family becomes cemented in this routine, and the children are the ones who suffer the most for it. They become engrossed in the shallow world of TV while their parents become accustomed to the convenience.

Who's minding the kids? If it's the TV, you'd better take a long, hard look at what it is doing to the precious children that God has entrusted to your care! "Until children are old enough to understand that television is fantasy—and, sadly many adults cannot even accomplish this task—young people are likely to be heavily influenced by the programming they view."[3]

Christian parents need to put the brakes on an every-day-and-night TV routine in their homes. If they park their kids in front of the tube, what kinds of messages are the kids receiving? First of all, your children will quickly learn that what their parents are doing is more important than spending time with them. Second, they will learn that watching TV is encouraged by their parents. And third, they will learn that *what* they are watching is approved by their parents.

Make no mistake—kids are sharp! Those messages are powerful in the mind and heart of a child. Children know that you restrict where they go and whom they associate with and when they must be home. If you turn them loose in front of the TV and say nothing more, they conclude, *My parents approve of this.* And you have, in essence! Later, when your children are old enough to make their own choices, they may well continue down that unfruitful path.

Bad Company

> In a sense, television functions as a "super peer group" with all the potential for influencing behavior that this entails.[4]

Christian parents monitor the company their kids keep and pray that they will choose godly friends. But all too often parents ignore one of the most powerful persuaders—television, the "Super Peer." Why worry about TV? For one thing, the average teenager views more than fourteen thousand sexual encounters *every year* on television, with adulterous relations outpacing marital ones by a margin of eight to one.[5]

Every year MTV takes its cameras to vacation beaches during spring break to capture footage of real-life college students engaging in every sort of debauchery. Egged on by celebrity hosts, students clad only in the skimpiest of swimsuits debase themselves in a variety of sexually suggestive antics—some of which involve stripping off all their clothing. Wise parents will pull the plug on this type of programming.

Christians should be cautioned against relying on a TV ratings system or V-chip to rescue their families from bad programming. Lax enforcement of the current movie ratings system demonstrates one problem with those approaches. In a survey of fifteen- and sixteen-year-olds in Michigan, more than half had seen a majority of the most popular R-rated movies either at the theater or on home VCRs.[6] So much for the law dictating that the content should be viewed by "no person under 17 unaccompanied by a parent."

Do not think for a minute that the video industry is innocent in this regard. Note for instance the elimination in 1990 of the taboo "X" rating from hard-core pornographic and grotesquely violent movies and videos. These brutal films now receive the innocuous-sounding "NC-17" rating. How many teens today are watching NC-17 films?

Sadly, many executives see TV and movie ratings systems as a ploy that allows producers to bring increasingly explicit fare into prime-time and daytime programming, so long as they merely slap a warning label on it. It opens the door even wider for the Super Peer—the one with the not-so-super morals.

Reading

> I read for one reason. . . . I read because my father had read to me.[7]

Few memories in my life carry as much emotional weight as reading time with my children. I recall my oldest son, at age three, grabbing my hand, pulling me towards his room, and begging, "Read me a book, Dad!" Lying together on his bed, Bosco Bear snuggled between us, we would crack open a book and immerse ourselves in the imaginative world of literature.

Over the years, I've read dozens of books to our kids—everything from Dr. Seuss and Winnie-the-Pooh to *The Book of Virtues* and Bible stories. Fascinated by lightning and thunder, our son Daniel would often request "the story where Jesus and his friends were in the boat and a *bad* storm came on the water. Would you read it, Dad, would you?"

When all is said and done, most of the world pays little attention to what Christian parents say or do. But our children watch us like hawks. My read-aloud skills could be better, truth be told, but my kids love every minute of it. I'm their dad; they're my best audience. Many times the book selection is a secondary consideration. They just want me.

Your children are not going to be readers, Mom and Dad, if you are not readers. They need you to read to them. You have to model it for them—reading good books, reading the newspaper, reading godly literature, and reading God's literature, the Bible. They need to know that you are a person of books and a person of *the* Book.

This skill of reading is something we have *learned*. It's quite unlike TV watching, which requires no effort or training at all. A two-year-old can space out in front of the tube just as easily as someone who's thirty-two—or ninety-two. Humans, though, must develop their reading ability. This skill must be diligently passed along to our children and grandchildren. We must live it; we must teach it.

But in America today a flood of messages on television, radio, and computers compete against reading time. In this environment, some people hardly read books, magazines, or newspapers at all! They are not *illiterate*—referring to those who *cannot* read. Perhaps we could call them *non-literate,* meaning that they *choose not* to read.

When the day's work is done, the non-literate rely on TV for news and almost never pick up a newspaper, magazine, or book. Aside from reading road signs and letters on *Wheel of Fortune,* they are not exposed to a whole lot of typographic stimuli. Sad to say, there may be followers of Christ included in this crowd, their minds and bodies turning into fluff in front of the glowing amusement tube.

People of *the* Book

> I have hidden your word in my heart that I might not sin against you. (Psalm 119:11)

One of the Bible's recurring themes is the importance of reading the Word. "Fix these words of mine in your hearts and minds. . . . Teach them to your children, talking about them when you sit at home and when you walk along the road, when you lie down and when you get up" (Deuteronomy 11:18-19).

Christians are to be devoted people of the Book—the Bible, God's Word. We are to read and meditate on the Word, use it as a lamp for our feet, a light for our path. Psalm 119 alone rejoices the heart with over one hundred verses encouraging us to dig into the wonderful Word of God.

However, a recent survey found that 75 percent of those who claim "strong" faith in Christ do not read their Bibles consistently.[8] One Christian joked that the greatest dust storm in history would occur if all the believers who have neglected their Bibles were to dust them off at the same time.

Yet the Word of God is much more than light devotional reading for the Christian. It is our weapon in the spiritual realm (Ephesians 6:17). There is a very real, life-and-death spiritual battle taking place in and around us every day. The Word of God is our sword; we need to pick it up and use it!

The Bible is also our accountability guidebook—detailing the requirements our Lord has set up for our lives. Yes, we are saved for eternity by grace through faith in Jesus Christ, period. But we will also be required to give an account for how we have invested our Christian lives. Jesus said, "Everyone who *hears* these words of mine and *puts them into practice* is like a wise man who built his house on the rock" (Matthew 7:24, emphasis added). We can't hear or act on words that we don't know!

There is no substitute for reading the Bible. Christian videos and music recordings have their place. Some of them are very good; some are of questionable quality. But watching and listening to Christian productions should never be more than a complement to the reading of God's Word. Parents should avoid the temptation to say, "My children don't really read the Bible, but they watch a lot of Christian videos," and let it go at that. That's not enough!

Children are not going to learn the practice of godly living primarily from kids' music recordings or cartoon video tapes. They need to read God's Word. Parents are not going to grow in faith from a Christian video diet that excludes Bible reading. The whole family needs God's Word.

Questions

1. Read the following Scripture passages. For each, explain how God instructs us to treat his Word; and describe the benefits for us and for others when we treat his Word as we should.

   Joshua 1:7-8

   Deuteronomy 4:5-10

   Revelation 1:1-3

2. Read the following passages in the book of Proverbs. For each, describe how God wants us to incorporate the Bible into our very lives.

   Proverbs 2:1-5

   Proverbs 3:1

Proverbs 4:4, 20-21

Proverbs 6:20-21

3. Read any eight-verse section of Psalm 119 (e.g., verses 105-112 or 137-144). List any synonyms for the Bible you find (e.g., commands, statutes, precepts, etc.).

4. If possible, spend some time with your family today. If you like, check Appendix A for some suggested activities.

5. Consider a read-through-the-Bible-in-one-year program. You may want to look for a *One Year Bible* at a Christian bookstore or contact a mail-order or online Christian book distributor. Mall bookstores and department store book sections often stock them.

6. Consider a pray-around-the-world program for yourself and/or your children. Operation Mobilisation publishes two wonderful books for this purpose: *Operation World* for adults and *You Can Change Your World* for children. Both are beautifully illustrated prayer guides for countries and people-groups across the globe. Order both from OM:

   OM Literature
   P.O. Box 1047
   Waynesboro, GA 30830
   1 8 MORE BOOKS (1 866 732 6657)–toll free
   (706) 554-5827
   Email: postmaster@omlit.om.org

CHAPTER FIVE

Did You See That?

*Above all else, guard your heart, for it is the
wellspring of life.*
—Proverbs 4:23

On May 9, 1961, the nation's top official in charge of
broadcasting concluded that American television was a "vast
wasteland." Newton Minow, President Kennedy's newly-
appointed communication chairman, scolded network
executives for their reckless pursuit of revenue and their
shameless appeal to baser interests.

"Watch a full day of your own programs," he challenged
them:

> You will see a procession of game shows, violence,
> audience participation shows, formula comedies about
> totally unbelievable families, blood and thunder,
> mayhem, violence, sadism, murder . . . and, endlessly,
> commercials—many screaming, cajoling, and
> offending. And most of all, boredom. True, you will
> see a few things you will enjoy. But they will be very,
> very few.[1]

It is amazing to think that these words were spoken four
decades ago, long before *NYPD Blue*, Howard Stern, and the

Playboy Channel; long before *Roseanne, South Park,* and
Saturday Night Live. Indeed the programming of yesteryear
seems breathtakingly tame compared to the "mayhem,
violence, and sadism" that spills out into America's homes
today via cable, satellite, and VCR.

During Minow's historic confrontation with broadcasters,
he specifically focused attention on the vulnerability of
viewing children. He lamented that most children spent as
much time watching television as they did at school:

> It used to be said that there were three great influences
> on a child: home, school, and church. Today there is a
> fourth great influence, and you ladies and gentlemen
> control it.[2]

And what an influence it is today. On any given
afternoon, 1.3 million kids, ages 12 to 17, are watching
Jerry Springer.[3] Jesus said that it would be better to have
an enormous stone hung around one's neck and be thrown
into the sea than to lead a child astray (Matthew 18:6).
Indeed, many TV executives will face serious
consequences for the destructive messages they deliver to
children. But what about the Christian parents who let
kids watch them?

Minow concluded that television's potential for good or
evil was unprecedented in human history. He urged
broadcasters to consider their "awesome responsibility" to
the audience. Unfortunately, the last forty years have
demonstrated all too clearly that TV executives have not
only ignored Minow's call to accountability, they have
spurned it.

The Language of Television

One of the clearest demonstrations of television's decline is its language. The vulgar graffiti of bathroom walls has become the dialogue of today's sitcoms, police dramas, and talk shows. Now even cartoons—once a reasonably safe domain for children—regularly feature trash-mouthed characters.

A sampling of the verbiage from a dozen prime-time shows in 1997–1998 shocks the conscience. A mere twelve programs included talking and jesting about urination, genitalia, sperm, orgies, transvestites, masturbation, prostitution, promiscuity, and bestiality. God's name was uttered in vain thirty-five times; profanities were spoken forty-one times.[4]

Remember, this is a description of just twelve individual programs, not a whole season of the shows, and these were taken only from the major networks: ABC, CBS, NBC, and FOX. Include programming available on cable, video rentals, and satellite, and TV's plunge into verbal depravity becomes even more disturbing.

Language is important in God's design for life! He sent His Son to earth as the *Word* of God. Jesus noted that one day he will require an answer for "every careless word" (Matthew 12:36). Psalm 141:3 counsels us to place the equivalent of an armed guard over our mouths because its potential for harm is so great. When the TV is on, we'd better guard our ears, too.

Channel Surfing . . . at the Dump?

Searching for positive, edifying programming on television today is often like rummaging through a garbage dump—it is very difficult to come up with anything of lasting value without getting badly soiled in the process. Often the product we come up with is so tainted by its environment or of such limited value that we should soberly question whether it was worth our time and distress. Some examples follow.

Surprise!

During a holiday visit with family, I awoke from a nap to hear the local TV news playing in the living room. A commercial for an upcoming network program interrupted. "Hold me, kiss me, make love to me!" a female character blurted. "Right here . . . right now!" This was *not* what young kids should be seeing at 6 P.M.

One mother told me about the commotion at her kids' middle school caused by just the *commercial* for a popular show. TV ads blared that the main characters—young teens—were going to lose their virginity on the next episode. It was the talk of the lunchroom and hallways, she said, even though many of the kids didn't watch the program; they just saw the ads!

Poor Sportsmanship

Sporting events often are punctuated with bodies, beer, and bad behavior. During the game, cameras zoom in on cheerleaders' skimpy outfits and shapely women in the crowd while commentators deliver thinly disguised innuendoes. Clever commercials for beer during ball games entice underage youth to drink. Sometimes "bad boys" of the game receive undue attention for their antics on and off the field or court.

What Happened to My Show?!

Some programs appear fairly tame early on, then make a rapid, dark turn to the pits. They introduce rude language, shocking story lines, and ungodly characters—sometimes after several seasons on the air.

Oh, No! They Used to Be So Good!
Similarly, stars of very fine programs move on to high-profile involvement in other detestable projects. For example, the lead actress in an uplifting film about teachers soon afterward debased herself in a highly publicized soft-porn film. It's risky to tune in to a show or rent a movie based on the earlier work of one of the stars. Even some veterans with whom we are all familiar have failed to keep their careers entirely on the wholesome road, steering instead into the immoral abyss.

Real Life Debauchery
Daytime talk shows roll out an endless parade of real people acting out the sexual sins of the TV age. Many air during "latchkey time" when kids are at home after school before their parents get home from work. Lists of perversions highlighted on *Ricki Lake*, *Jerry Springer*, and the like are too sordid to mention, much less watch!

MTV recruited young people to live together in a house so that they could be videotaped damaging their lives—for a television program. Now several networks are racing to put real people in dangerous, confrontational, and sexually suggestive situations, taking them to deserted islands, the Australian outback, and other locales, all in the name of entertainment. One wonders if we are living in a dying society, one that has taken leave of its senses.

Same Wavelength

One doesn't have to look very hard to find Satan's fingerprints all over many awful shows. There is no human conspiracy driving the barrage of regrettable programming on TV—no secret Trilateral Television Commission, no Hooded Order of Evil TV Execs. Television's decline is simply a matter of sinful people creating terrible entertainment in a world of crumbling morals.

King David noted that we come forth from the womb sinful—all of us (Psalm 51:5). No one had to send today's top movie and television producers to the Academy of the Awful. They produce and promote godless products naturally. The unsaved person is at enmity—at war—with God. And we're all in the same boat! Apart from Christ, if we lived and worked in that world, we would be just as capable of devoting our skills to produce the same sort of rotten fare.

Unfortunately, many of the power brokers of today's entertainment industry clearly operate on the same wavelength. That is why their work is so consistently sinful. Often, when movie and TV execs find others who support the same immoral causes or wayward political agendas, they join forces. This sort of collaboration is far from new; the very day that Jesus Christ was being deprived of justice in early Palestine, "Herod and Pilate became friends—before this they had been enemies" (Luke 23:12).

Sadly, many who produce programs have demonstrated their passion for pushing the envelope with objectionable material. In 1992, the three major networks demonstrated their concept of an "ideal" TV news story: A man who lived in Long Island, New York, was having an adulterous relationship with a seventeen-year-old girl who ran a prostitution ring at her high school. In an attempt to keep the man, the teen shot the man's wife in the head. Horrible, you say? Not in the eyes of TV executives! CBS, NBC, and ABC *all* rushed to produce made-for-TV versions of the sordid tale.[5] "Having lost all sensitivity, they have given themselves over to sensuality so as to indulge in every kind of impurity, with a continual lust for more" (Ephesians 4:19).

"Fools mock at making amends for sin," Proverbs 14:9 tells us. So do the masters of television. Media critic Michael Medved has identified the Three Big Lies that the entertainment empire uses to justify its continuing depravity:

Lie #1—It's Only Entertainment; It Doesn't Influence Anybody

Advertisers wouldn't be paying multiple millions of dollars airing commercials and supporting programs that influenced no one. Networks wouldn't be pulling out all the stops to increase their shows' ratings if it truly were "only entertainment."

Lie #2—We Just Reflect Reality. Don't Blame Us, Blame Society.

Medved notes that about 7 of the approximately 350 characters appearing on primetime television each evening are murdered. If this homicide rate reflected the real world, then in less than two months every person in America would be killed, and "the last left could turn off the TV."

Lie #3—We Give the Public What It Wants. If People Don't Like It, They Can Always Turn It Off.

For over two decades, G- and PG-rated films for family audiences have earned twice the amount of money as

R-rated films. But instead of increasing production of lower-rated films, Hollywood has upped the number of R-rated films to nearly two-thirds of all releases. Many of these R titles never even earn a profit for their producers. The continuing production of such films shows the careful observer a motion picture industry that cares little for traditional families and their values.[6]

In a day and age when those in control of what is broadcast to the nation have no restraint, the heads of Christian households must. Do we think that it is all right to lower our standards because the world has lowered its own? The people of Christ's church are supposed to be salt and light to the earth, to have a powerful impact on humankind, not the other way around! It will take great effort, but believers need to take a stand against this onslaught of detrimental material.

God's Word is abundantly clear: "Get rid of all moral filth" (James 1:21). "Abstain from sinful desires, which war against your soul" (1 Peter 2:11). "Have nothing to do with the fruitless deeds of darkness. . . . For it is shameful even to mention what the disobedient do in secret" (Ephesians 5:11-12).

Forty years ago, Newton Minow spoke of the tremendous power of a medium that only broadcast programs from 6 A.M. to midnight on three networks. Today, hundreds of stations on antenna, cable, and satellite deliver messages 24 hours a day, 365 days a year, all around the world. Television programming is far more than a "vast wasteland" now. It's a battlefield for the minds of millions.

Questions

1. Read the following Scriptures. For each, describe the importance God places on spoken language.

   Proverbs 25:11

   James 1:26

   Matthew 12:33-37

   Genesis 1:3

   Proverbs 10:11

   Ephesians 4:25, 29

2. Read the following Scriptures. Describe how each relates to the flood of negative programming on television.

Matthew 15:19-20

Galatians 6:7-8

2 Timothy 3:1-5

Matthew 13:22

Mark 13:32-37

CHAPTER SIX

Entertainment and News

*"He died for all, that those who live should
no longer live for themselves but for him
who died for them."*

—2 Corinthians 5:15

Disposable income. Free time. These interesting terms have
become popular descriptors of contemporary America.
According to scholars, a nation must have both extra money
and extra time to support media institutions. These, along
with a large population and technological know-how, allow
citizens to regularly invest part of their lives in media
consumption.

But the ideas of *disposable income* and *free time* pose
serious challenges to Christ's parables regarding
stewardship. Jesus demonstrated that those who squandered
money and time suffered eternal consequences. Consider
the parable of the man who buried his talent in the ground
(Matthew 25:14-30) or the one who dreamed of building
bigger barns and taking life easy (Luke 12:16-21).

In Revelation we see the church in the city of Laodicea
populated by those considered "rich and well-fed and in
need of nothing" (Revelation 3:17). Sound familiar? With
the right technology, Laodicea too could have supported a
booming media empire! But Christ also said they had

become lukewarm toward God! Is the same true of the church in America today?

Labor-saving machinery during the late 1800s brought higher wages, shorter work weeks, and the *Penny Press*—a big daily newspaper costing one cent. This paper for the masses was followed by motion pictures, radio, and television.

From the beginning, many "mass" media appealed to the desire for entertainment. Some turn-of-the-century "news"-papers found they could increase circulation if they produced sensationalized stories, heavy on violence and sex, light on facts.

Early movies and radio also strove to entertain audiences with shoot-'em-ups and comedies. Television followed suit. In fact, most TV programming is entertainment, packaged in a variety of forms. Today's dramas, comedies, talk shows, advertisements—even news shows—are created to attract and amuse audiences.

The Value of Entertainment

Our family has found, if we are very selective, that quality entertainment programming can be both enjoyable and edifying in modest doses. My wife and I occasionally like to watch a plot-twisting adventure or stirring drama. Our children enjoy classic cartoon films, family comedies, and animal shows. We all love Adventures in Odyssey, Focus on the Family's excellent audio and video series.

It's therapeutic to have a good laugh now and then, to cultivate a healthy sense of humor. Sometimes a funny video just hits the spot! And dramas that tastefully deal with the trying times and thorny issues of human experience can stir us to compassion or help us make important changes in our lives.

But moderation is important. Anything can be done to death, even if it is delicious food or vacation travel or holiday gifts . . . or entertainment.

Complacent in Zion

Many followers of Jesus Christ have concluded that it's perfectly okay for them to devote large blocks of time almost every day to entertaining themselves. I am not speaking here of a walk with the family or an evening out with a spouse. Those involve healthy recreation and family time. I am referring to the unabashed pursuit of a self-gratifying experience of some kind—thumbing through an unedifying magazine, renting a questionable video, or watching hours of mindless television programming.

The Lord of the Sabbath knows that his people need rest. Jesus even encouraged his disciples at one point to come away with him for a time of renewal. But in God's Word "woe" was pronounced on those who were perpetually "complacent in Zion," demonstrating little concern for their nation's sins. They lounged on ivory-trimmed couches, Amos lamented, dining on choice food and drink, listening to music, and smoothing on lotions. All of this while the people turned from God (Amos 6:1-8).

Are there any biblical examples of godly people relentlessly seeking entertainment? Christ ate dinner with some pretty questionable characters. But as he spent time with sinners, he used it as an opportunity for ministry, not to partake in their revelry.

Historians believe Paul spent his "free time" making tents

to financially support his ministry, as did Priscilla and Aquila. In Acts chapter 9 Dorcas made clothes for fellow Christians. Peter and John invested countless hours sharing messages about Christ, organizing ministry trips, going to the house of God to preach and pray, and working to meet others' needs. When we get to heaven, we can ask them if they found their lives boring or in need of entertainment.

Who, then, in biblical accounts *did* spend their time pursuing entertainment without restraint? More often than not, it was the less-than-godly. Herod commissioned his wife's daughter to dance for his party guests (Matthew 14:6-7). I imagine she dazzled them with a swirling, seductive romp set to music, something akin to an ancient music video. In the book of Esther, King Xerxes gave a weeklong banquet flowing with wine; he also collected a harem of women for his pleasure (Esther 1:7; 2:2). Daniel confronted Belshazzar, king of Babylon, for defiling the temple goblets during a drunken feast (Daniel 5:23).

It appears that accounts of entertainment excess in the Word of God most often involve wealthy people pursuing seductive pleasure—people with plenty of *disposable income* and *free time*. Solomon pursued pleasure unabashedly, but it cost him dearly. He joined himself to many foreign wives who eventually "led him astray" (1 Kings 11:3). What a startling statement about the man who at one time was called "wiser than any other man" (1 Kings 4:29-34).

Selfish Time

Television has become so pervasive, so accepted, in our society that it may be difficult to think of it as a doorway to self-centered entertainment. But what if the man or woman of the house immersed themselves just as zealously in some other form of entertainment? What if he was a Monopoly junkie or she was hooked on some electronic game?

Consider the hypothetical reactions of two spouses:

Kirk sighs, "Jeannie spends all her free time reading racy novels and women's magazines. I know it's not good for her."

Karen complains, "Jim comes home after work every night of the week and spends at least three or four hours playing pinball. He eats dinner in front of it, and I can hardly get him away from that machine to talk to me or the children. Most Saturday and Sunday afternoons that's all he does!"

What would you think if your spouse or neighbor or pastor were addicted to video games or bad books? Is mindless devotion to TV any better?

The Death of Discretion

Through most of television's first two decades, open discussions about sex were all but unknown, with the exception of "occasional discrete references" on adult drama programs.[1] Instead, good-natured variety shows such as Milton Berle's *Texaco Star Theatre*, family comedies like *The Life of Riley*, and wholesome Westerns such as *The Lone Ranger* prevailed.

However, during the late 1960s and through the 1970s, the floodgates opened. Researcher S. Robert Lichter and his associates—who conducted a thorough content analysis of TV shows from 1955 to 1986—note the introduction of many previously taboo subjects during that time. Comedy shows featured bikini dancers, striptease routines, and embarrassing honeymoon intimacy; sitcoms spouted sexual innuendoes and *doubles entendres*; dramas featured detailed discussions of teen sex, adultery, impotence, and abortion. Dubbing TV programming in that era the "raunch race," Lichter and associates note that "[t]hroughout the rest of the 1970s, almost anything could happen in the willy-nilly race toward new frontiers of titillation."[2]

What did the researchers' data discover about TV programs *since* the 1970s? "Recent seasons have offered viewers incest, child prostitution, kiddie porn, a variety of fetishes, transvestites, sadomasochism, and bestiality."[3]

The researchers also noted *how* sexual encounters have been portrayed:

"On the TV screen, sex is usually without consequence, without worry, and with rarely a bad experience."

- "Today most forms of sexual behavior are either taken for granted or treated as legitimate choices of personal lifestyle. Extramarital sex, adultery, homosexuality, pornography, and prostitution have all lost their taboo status."

- Homosexuals "made a transition 'from invisibility to saturation' as popular sitcoms like *Alice* and *Barney Miller* introduced recurring homosexual characters. Equally important, most scripts on gay themes were reviewed by the Gay Media Task Force, which sought to eliminate negative stereotypes such as effeminate mannerisms."

- "A notable shift in recent years is to show extramarital sex as a fact of life. . . . Since [the 1970s] it's been taken for granted as a form of recreation with no moral or even emotional consequences."[4]

Television now promotes a lineup of programs with graphic sexual encounters. Cable programs routinely feature complete male and female nudity and a full range of sexual sins. Even an *advertisement* during a recent Super Bowl clearly displayed persons having sex. The discretion of the 1950s is gone—and television helped kill it. Every variety of sexual behavior is on worldwide display with no shame and no attempt to hide it.

What does all this mean for Christians? For one, those who have trouble with lustful thoughts should not keep feeding that desire with TV. Men should avoid raunchy sitcoms and steamy films with loose women. Women should forego romantic screen stories that go way too far. Teens with raging hormones should not watch sexually suggestive programming lest they be nudged into sin.

Watching seductive shows is like putting a Big Mac dispenser in the living room of a man who eats too much fast food. When he turns it on, he doesn't expect yogurt and spinach salad to pop out. He's going to get calories and cholesterol, and he knows it.

Christians cannot sit back and expect TV producers to stop pumping out their prurient products. Media producers are not innocent bystanders in this process. Most have long since established what kind of message they are going to put on your set—*if you let them*! But you don't have to! It's *your* home, isn't it? Then guess who has the responsibility before God for monitoring TV viewing in your home? You do!

Nor should Christians rely on guidance from secular "critics" of popular culture. *USA Today* reviewed one video for their weekend edition. "It's tacky, tasteless, and trashy," the review said. "It also has more naked breasts than a Perdue chicken factory." The article concluded that readers should "sneak into a video store" and rent it.[5]

Christ said a "tree is recognized by its own fruit" (Luke 6:44). Bad apples have proliferated on the TV tree for many years. And don't expect TV's crop to get dramatically better in the future. "Because of the increase of wickedness, the love of most will grow cold," Jesus said of the end times (Matthew 24:12). That intensifying wickedness is all too clear on television.

A few years ago, a decisive moment came for the Brown family. Their disgust with the river of offensive material on television came to a head one night while watching a sitcom with their two school-age daughters. A curvaceous woman seductively approached the main character—a husband and father—announcing that she was "his birthday present." That was it! Not wanting their girls bombarded with the message that women are "sex objects" for men, the Browns sold their TV and have never looked back. They regularly remark how much happier they have been without it!

Breaking the News

Pause for a moment and recall some of the big news stories of the last decade: adultery in politics; a woman dismembering her husband; celebrities committing violent crimes; athletes taking bribes, doing drugs, and contracting diseases. Do we really need to hear the gritty details of all these tragedies night after night?

Feeling the pressure from daily deadlines and the competitive desire to be the first to "break" the news, some reporters will run with a story before they have all the facts.

They forget that people's careers and families can be ruined by false information—even if it is retracted later.

God's Word says that it is foolish and shameful for people to answer a matter before hearing the whole story (Proverbs 18:13). We are also told that the foolish person "finds no pleasure in understanding but delights in airing his own opinions" (Proverbs 18:2). Yet in spite of God's wise instructions, TV newscasts often feature superficial and misleading stories.

A recent study by the American Society of Newspaper Editors demonstrates the public's general disgust with television and print news organizations:

- 78 percent of those polled said the news media are "biased and unfair"

- 80 percent believed news coverage is determined by how sensational a news story is, not by its relevance

- 45 percent said a story should *not* run if it's attributed to anonymous sources[6]

On television, every news story has to have a *picture* or it dies. And TV news is predominately negative—good deeds seldom attract the camera's attention. As one journalist quipped, "If it bleeds, it leads."

Television news is not a very efficient time investment either. The typical evening newscast contains twenty-two minutes of visually oriented content and eight minutes of commercials. The printed transcript of an entire nightly news show wouldn't fill the front page of the typical daily paper; an entire week of TV news stories wouldn't fill the first section.

A study of local television news from sixty-one stations in twenty cities noted the following:

Short Stories
Seventy percent of the news stories were less than one minute long; 43 percent lasted 30 seconds or less; only 16 percent of the stories were longer than 2 minutes.[7] It's impossible to cover a news topic properly when the stories are barely longer than the commercials!

Canned Stories
Almost half of the stories were based on events that were "prearranged or staged," such as community happenings, news conferences, jury trials, and stock market reports. In 20 percent of those stories, the station did not even have a reporter at the scene of the event! Another 15 percent of local news coverage consisted of video footage from other news organizations, such as CNN or the networks.[8]

Single Source Stories
Only one-quarter of the stories used two or more sources. The rest relied on only one named source or did not name a source at all! A strong case for bias can be made against news that only tells one side of the story.

> In stories that involved disputable information, viewers were just as likely to get only one side as to get a mix of views. . . . This finding is especially troubling, since past research of both network and print news has suggested that above all else, journalists make sure that they at least offer a balance of views.[9]

Poor Quality News Overall

A similar study found that many TV news stations took "superficial and reactive" approaches to their reporting and called the result "journalism on the run." It further found that "at most stations reporters are required to produce more than a story a day—a demand that makes depth and care difficult if not impossible."[10]

How many items of major importance, of real consequence, do you miss when you turn off the TV news? Actually, you will miss many unsettling stories that are completely unnecessary. You'll also miss an awful lot of promotional hype for stars and shows and events.

The argument that you "won't know what's going on in the world" without TV news doesn't pass muster—particularly if you turn to quality print or radio news sources instead.

What secular TV news programs do *not* tell you are the exciting stories of how the gospel is spreading in Cuba, in China, and in Muslim North Africa. They don't tell you how Christians in the Middle East and Asia are suffering . . . and how badly they need our prayers. Between May 1998 and May 1999 in Indonesia, for example, ninety-five Christian churches were burned.[11] As I write this, I am looking at a picture of some of our dedicated Indonesian brothers and sisters in the Lord worshiping God in the rain at the site of their burned-out building. How many TV channels do you think covered that story on the evening news?

Want to know what is really going on in the nation's capital or state capital? Tune in to a good Christian radio station or buy a quality newspaper. Want to know what is happening in the countries where our Lord's missionaries are serving? Request newsletters from mission agencies and citizens organizations. Visit the Web sites of well-respected ministries (see Appendix B for more information). You will discover a wealth of timely information and uplifting material.

Questions

1. Read Revelation 3:14-19. How does the church of Laodicea compare with the church of America today?

2. Read the following passages of Scripture. For each, describe the actions of leaders during times of leisure.

   Matthew 14:6-7

   Daniel 5:1-4

2 Samuel 11:1-4

Amos 6:1-7

1 Kings 11:1-9

3. Read the following Scripture passages and explain what each says about those who are "complacent."

Luke 12:16-21

Isaiah 32:9-11

Jeremiah 48:11

Zechariah 1:15

Proverbs 6:6-11

2 Thessalonians 3:6-13

Zephaniah 1:12

4. Are you familiar with all of the Christian radio stations in your area? If not, you may want to spend some time searching along the AM and FM dial to see what kind of music and programming are available. If you locate some stations, you may want to listen to their newscasts, usually broadcast on the hour.

CHAPTER SEVEN

Choices

The machine in question does not operate automatically; neither does its programming enter your home uninvited. The reason that television has such a large sphere of influence in our society and in our lives is that we enter into a sort of "relationship" with it. To argue that hours of daily television viewing in your home "just happen" is like Aaron's explanation to Moses about the golden calf: "They gave me the gold, and I threw it into the fire, and out came this calf!" (Exodus 32:24). To hear some Christians explain it, they just sat down in the living room, the TV turned on all by itself, and out came violent men, nearly-naked women, and vulgar language.

But you *chose* television. You earned the money and checked the prices. You drove to the store, purchased a set, and moved furniture at home to get a better view of it. You plugged it in, turned it on, and adjusted the picture. Wanting better reception and more selections, you called the cable or satellite company, bought a VCR, and rented videos.

You have invited this guest into your home. *Invited!* How has this guest been treated? You've given it a prime spot in the center of your house. You've given it access to your mind and to your kids' minds for hours on end, 365 days a year. And every day you watch, you make choices between television and family time, television and quiet time, television and productive time.

Choices and Consequences

Not long ago, a few miles from our home, a twelve-year-old boy riding his bike was hit by a car. It ended his life. Shocked by the incident, I talked with a neighbor who said the boy often shot out of his driveway into a blind curve in the road. Immersed in this dangerous routine and undeterred by the warnings of his parents, it was just a matter of time before he suffered a tragic accident.

The brutal reality of life is this: Many childhood lessons have consequences of life-and-death proportion. There's no "you'll do better next time" for the child who jumps into a swift river that overwhelms his or her best swim stroke. There is no "second chance" for the youth who ingests a lethal dose of drugs.

Somehow, though, many Christians who have mastered the hard lessons of childhood often drop their guard as they make their way into and through adulthood. It's a costly mistake. Yes, Jesus paid the eternal penalty for sin, and God forgives. But choices still have consequences, some irreversible. For example, we are told that the man who commits adultery in some ways "destroys himself," that "his shame will never be wiped away" fully, and that the woman's husband "will not accept any compensation" (Proverbs 6:32-35).

This world presents a continuous series of critical choices

with consequences that carry on into eternity. Yet Christians are often swayed in their decision making by the rivers of seemingly trivial media messages they drink in over the years. Habitually shooting out into the blind curves of life, they too are immersed in a dangerous routine. In time the video messages that fill their minds and captivate their hearts will steer their wills. "The mind of sinful man is death, but the mind controlled by the Spirit is life and peace" (Romans 8:6).

A mind overflowing with deceptive and erroneous media messages can cause an otherwise dependable Christian to misstep. In life's crucial decision-making moments, his or her mind may flash back to the evening soaps that glamorize adultery, or the beer advertisements that mimic true fellowship, or the sitcoms that cloud moral standards.

Those Who Have Much

Sometimes as I make my way through the burgeoning salad, dinner, and dessert bar at a local restaurant, I am overwhelmed and humbled. "Lord, thank you for all of this food," I pray. "Let me never take it for granted."

Never in the history of the world have Christians in any nation been blessed with as many resources—freedom, money, and time—as we have today! We have an abundance that believers of the past would marvel at: a cornucopia of food beyond description; conveniences for every facet of daily life; remarkable medical advances; unfettered transportation by land, sea, and air to every corner of the earth; instant global communication by word, voice, and image.

Jesus said that from those believers "who have been given much, much will be demanded" (Luke 12:48). Hey! That's *us*! Clearly God did not give us all of this abundance just so that we could indulge ourselves. Our Savior did not die so that we could sit in a recliner and watch television while the needs of our family and our world cry out for attention. We need to be shaking the world for Christ. Television executives are playing for keeps. Isn't it time Christian parents and families responded in like manner?

Have Some Backbone!

Fred has a regular visitor to his home that mistreats his kids, discourages his wife, uses filthy language, and *flaunts* it. Fred knows that he should control this intruder, but he just shrugs his shoulders and claims there's nothing much he can do about it!

In many Christian homes, TV has become just such an intruder. If you know that your relationship with television is not what it should be, don't be a wimp like Fred. *Do* something about it!

Before tangible solutions are offered, however, let's review some potential stumbling blocks—excuses often used to justify uncontrolled TV watching.

There Are Some Really Good Shows on TV

Yes, indeed there are some. But are those the programs you and your family are *actually* watching day-in and day-out? Is it symphony concerts and "The Life of the Mollusk," or is it mindless comedies and R-rated cable movies?

What Will I Talk About with Friends at Work?

If you need three hours of sports to prepare for three minutes of conversation with the folks at work, something is wrong. Adults shake their heads at the crazy dilemmas teens get themselves into with peer pressure. What about you? There's nothing wrong with saying, "I didn't watch the game; I was playing ball with my own kids."

I Need to Keep Up with What's Going On
Christians who rely heavily on television news to shape their worldview may be misinformed. The world according to CBS, CNN, and the local TV news could be a far cry from what the Lord would have us focus on. Take some initiative, and search for quality news on the radio, in print, and on the Internet.

I Need to See the Weather Report
Why sit through thirty minutes of mayhem, trivia, and commercials for a few seconds of weather on the local TV news? That's not always a good return on your investment of time. Try radio, newspaper, Internet, or dial-up weather reports.

I Watch Because It Relates to What I Do
It's hard to justify fourteen consecutive weekends of nonstop sports simply because you're serving as assistant coach for the Little League Tigers.

And what about information for your career? Read magazines and newsletters specific to your industry and interests. Look up Internet sites related to your field.

I Don't Want to *Overdo* It; I'll Just Cut Back a *Little* Here and There
Will two weeks of toned-down viewing quickly return to the same old routine? One parent commented, "The turnoff was great—we did so many things together—we really felt

much more like a real family. But somehow or other we've slowly but surely drifted back to watching the same way we always did—too much."[1]

And perhaps the most seductive justification of all. . .

Everybody *Else* at Church Is Watching a Lot of TV, and They Don't Seem to Be That Concerned about It

A steady diet of television can't be all that bad if so many Christians today are doing it, right? Well, consider that God confronted the whole *nation* of Israel—his chosen people— time and again for their sins. Christ labeled an entire generation "adulterous and sinful" (Mark 8:38). Just because "everybody's doing it" doesn't make it right!

Imagine the sight on the Day of judgment, standing amidst a crowd beyond number—the sea of humanity from around the globe and across the centuries. Yet only those people who have lived since 1950 in the world's richest nations have devoted so much to TV. The rest of mankind will be astonished as your life is replayed: "You watched *that* in your home . . . for *how* many years of your life?"

Make the Change

During their toddler years, all three of our children tried to climb up playground ladders or into chairs with toys held tightly in their hands. It took some persistence to persuade them that they needed to let go of the toy and use both hands to succeed. Many Christians are like spiritual toddlers, trying to climb the ladder of life with a tight grip on their televisions.

It's time to grow up in the Lord. Now is the time to "let

go" of unrestrained television viewing and live for God fully. "Therefore, since we are surrounded by such a great cloud of witnesses, let us throw off everything that hinders and the sin that so easily entangles, and let us run with perseverance the race marked out for us" (Hebrews 12:1).

You won't win a popularity contest for making a strategic move with television in your house. The longer your kids have had free reign with the TV, the harder it's going to be for them to get used to the idea of cutting back or going without. Your spouse may not be thrilled about it either. Neighbors may smirk. Expect some opposition at first, but expect results from God as well!

Some will applaud and encourage you, and you may inspire others to take up the challenge. With or without support from the larger community, God will help you say no to excessive TV watching. "For the grace of God that brings salvation has appeared to all men. It teaches us to say 'No' to ungodliness and worldly passions, and to live self-controlled, upright and godly lives in this present age" (Titus 2:11-12).

Olympic athletes say no to rich foods and sleeping in. Soldiers in battle carry only the essentials in their packs and sleep on the ground. They make sacrifices for their goals. Christians, what sort of extraneous gear are we toting around? We ought to pull everything out of our daily backpacks and then justify each one as "essential" before putting it back in. This is a great way to continue your fast from television! Keep it locked away and do not turn it back on until you can *justify* each program watched, each hour spent. If it stays in the garage until Christ returns, that's okay.

How important are the goals of a godly life and a

Christian family? We are living toward a prize: eternal life. We are at war, a spiritual war of great proportions. It is time for sacrifices to be made.

Three Options

As your TV-free week draws to a close, it is vitally important that you ask God for guidance: *Lord, what do you want me to do with television?* Here are three options to prayerfully consider.

Option #1: No Television

No TV at all. And while it may sound boring, TV-free families don't just "survive" without the goggle box, they *thrive!* You'll be amazed at the newfound joy and creativity of your kids, the peaceful atmosphere in your home, and the productive endeavors that fill your evenings and weekends. People will not stop and point at you on the street because you put your television away. Some may well salute you, saying, "We ought to try that!"

You and your kids will not be "deprived" of anything. In fact, if you invest more time in your kids' lives, they will begin to enjoy many family blessings they had been missing before. Make the tough choice! You will be glad you did.

Our family lived without a television set for several years. Boy, did we enjoy the peace and quiet! The Lord encourages us to "be still, and know that I am God" (Psalm 46:10). You can do this in a TV-free home with no firing guns or shouting actors disturbing you. Evenings will be free for family, not dictated by "what's on" at 9 P.M. Read books to the kids, talk with your spouse, or go for a walk.

Fill your free time with reading and Christian radio,

ministry and good music, friendships and fellowship, exercise and outings. You might be less "entertained," but you will be much more edified, enriched, and informed!

Option #2: Just a TV and VCR

No cable, no satellite, and no antenna. Reserve TV for wholesome videos you select. Careful, selective viewing makes the programs you *do* watch more enjoyable and rewarding! The saying "Less is more" definitely applies to television. You can store your TV/VCR in a closet or behind closed cabinet doors and only watch during prearranged family viewing times.

If you had cable or satellite, send the money you save each month to a missionary. Families that prayerfully make this sacrifice will reap lasting blessings from the decision.

Option #3: Selective Viewing

Wholesome videos, select cable channels, and carefully monitored TV viewing. This is a very difficult option because of the enormous temptation to slip back into excessive viewing. It requires remarkable diligence to maintain. The upside is that you can take advantage of some good programming. However, if you drift back into the TV trap, try option #1 or #2.

Other Strategies to Consider

No TV during Daylight Hours

Kids and adults of all ages can enjoy outdoor activities during daylight hours. If it's cold or rainy, pull out some good books! This one works great on vacations, too.

Daily Time with TV Not to Exceed Time Spent with the Lord

When an early meeting or sleeping in causes you to miss your quiet time, you can make it up in the evening instead of engaging in mindless TV viewing.

Make Some Notes

If you do watch, take note of how and why you watch. How do you use TV—or how does it use you? Store a notepad next to your chair in the living room. Keep a record of the shows you watch, the time you spend, and, most important, the thoughts and temptations with which you wrestle.

Get a sense for *why* you watched what you watched. Be honest. *I like to watch this sitcom because the costar is an attractive woman who wears tight/low-cut blouses—better skip this one from now on. I watched this ballgame so I could talk with my coworkers about it tomorrow. I should have been helping my wife.*

Put the Set behind Doors

Buy a cabinet for your TV. Help your family rearrange the living-room furniture to accommodate people instead of just a boob tube surrounded by gawking chairs. Does a television set need to be the centerpiece or focal point in your living room, family room, or bedroom?

Unplug the Drug

Can't seem to turn it off when you should? Put it in a closet when you are not using it. This can be a very effective deterrent to wasteful watching. If you have a console that won't move, sell it (or store it), and buy a portable.

When You Decide to Watch Television Together, *Talk* to Your Family about Questionable Programming

"That was really unnecessary language." "They didn't need to show that." "Let's turn this off or change the channel." "I'm not sure we need to watch this."

Place a Prominent Scripture Card on the Top or Front of the Television

A hastily-scribbled verse on notebook paper may not match the living-room decor, so design and create a Scripture placard everyone can live with. Suggestions: Proverbs 4:23-24; Job 31:1. Read the passages carefully, and spend a moment in prayer before turning on the TV.

Questions

1. Read the following Scriptures. What does each passage suggest about preparing for the future?

   Matthew 16:2-3

   1 Chronicles 12:32

Jonah 3:4-6

Ezekiel 33:1-6

Genesis 6:22

1 Corinthians 7:29-31

Matthew 24:44

2. Now that you have lived a week without it, please describe your previous relationship with television. (Not really bad, but could be a lot better? heavily dependent? prone to weekend marathon viewing? sports-a-holic? sitcom junkie? soap opera groupie?)

3. Read the following Scriptures. For each, explain how it can relate to the viewing of television by Christians.

Hebrews 12:1-2

Matthew 7:13-14

1 Corinthians 9:24-27

2 Timothy 2:20-21

1 John 2:15-17

James 4:17

4. Answer the following questions regarding your television viewing.

   a. Have you been watching TV at times when you believe the Lord would *not* want you to? If so, describe them.

   b. Do you believe God would have you decrease your television viewing? Why?

   c. If you answered yes to questions a and b above, then describe specifically *how* you are going to decrease television viewing in your home. You may want to review some of the options described in this chapter.

   d. If you answered yes to questions a and b above, then *set a date* when you will decrease or cease television viewing in your home.
   Date _____ Time _____

   e. If you were not sure how to answer a and b above, then you may want to read 1 Thessalonians 5:21-22 and pray earnestly, "God, what would *you* have me do with television viewing in my life and in our home?"

TV-Free Activities to Enrich Your Life

- Read a book. Read to someone else.
- Go to the library and check out some good books.
- Take an early morning walk and talk to God.
- Write a letter to a friend.
- Read the Bible. Start a One Year reading program.
- Ride a bike. Ride a bike to work or school.
- Bake cookies or bread. Share with a neighbor.
- Go fishing. Take some kids fishing.
- Plant a garden. Fix something.
- Organize a trip to visit folks at a nursing home.
- Learn some simple phrases in Spanish.
- Enjoy a moment of silence. Take a nap.
- Invite a coworker, friend, or neighbor to church.
- Write or type a detailed prayer list. Pray through it.
- Plan a picnic or barbecue.
- Read a bedtime Bible story to your kids.

- Walk the dog. Wash the dog.
- Start a diary or journal.
- Paint a picture. Paint a room.
- Go swimming.
- Listen to some music: Gospel, classical, bluegrass.
- Attend a community concert. Join your church choir.
- Take a trip by bus or train.
- Go to a ball game.
- Have a yard sale. Donate the money to missions.
- Play hide-and-seek, hopscotch, or freeze tag with your kids.
- Catch fireflies at dusk.
- Write or E-mail a missionary. Send them a package.
- Make crafts to give as gifts.
- Give your spouse and kids a hug.
- Build a model airplane with your family.
- Mow the lawn at church. Mow your pastor's lawn.
- Play a board game with family or friends.
- Climb a tree. Watch the sunset.
- Read a good Christian book. Listen to a book on tape.
- Make your own pizza.
- Learn to play a musical instrument.
- Start a weekly Bible study with your spouse.
- Have a cup of coffee and a conversation.
- Visit a zoo or pet store.

- Wake up early and make pancakes or waffles.
- Make your own greeting cards for birthdays/holidays.
- Take your kids camping. Tell stories around the campfire.
- Build a fort in the living room.
- Go fly a kite. (This is FUN!)
- Play checkers, chess, or bridge.
- Visit a Christian bookstore.
- Repair or refinish a piece of furniture.
- Join an activity at the community center or park.
- Research your family history and draw a family tree.
- Take your family out for ice cream.
- Shoot hoops with a friend. Play a game of HORSE.
- Call your mom and tell her you love her.

Ministry Information

> *I tell you, open your eyes and look at the*
> *fields! They are ripe for harvest.*
> —John 4:35.

Our first ministry priorities as Christians, after our families, are to our local churches—to tithe and prayerfully support their ministries and missionaries. My prayer is that, having used this guidebook throughout your TV-free week, you may desire to direct energy away from unproductive TV time and toward those to whom this book is dedicated. Below are listed a number of exciting ministries that you may wish to learn about, pray for, give to, and assist.

The Gospel by Radio to All Peoples

Four radio ministries began working together in September 1985 on the "World by Radio" project to help "provide every man, woman, and child on earth the opportunity to turn on their radio and hear the gospel of Jesus Christ in a language they can understand, so that they can become followers of Christ and responsible members of his church." Over the past fifteen years, these four ministries have developed gospel programs for shortwave radio broadcast in over 150 of the world's "megalanguages."

Visit the Web sites of these ministries, or call, or write;

ask for their newsletters. Read incredible, uplifting letters from listeners who have come to know the Lord in Asia, Africa, South America, and elsewhere. See their remarkable lists of broadcast languages.

Far East Broadcasting Company

Address: P.O. Box 1
La Mirada, CA 90637-0001
Web site: www.febc.org
E-mail: info@febc.org

Request the *Prayer Target* monthly prayer guide and *Broadcaster* magazine.

HCJB World Radio

Address: P.O. Box 39800
Colorado Springs, CO 80949
Phone: 719-590-9800
Web site: www.hcjb.org
E-mail: info@hcjb.org

Request their newsletter. The call letters HCJB stand for Heralding Christ Jesus' Blessings.

SIM Missionary Radio

Address: P.O. Box 6900
Charlotte, NC 28241
Phone: 800-521-6449
Web site: www.sim.org
E-mail: chris.wade@sim.org; ralph@webmail.sim.org

Ask for *SIM NOW* magazine. SIM began as Sudan Interior Missions, then expanded to include missionary and radio ministries throughout the African continent.

Trans World Radio

Address: Box 8700
            Cary, NC 27512
Phone: 800-456-7897; 919-460-3700
Web site: www.twr.org

Request *Trans World Radio* magazine and the E-mail newsletter *E-Snapshots.*

Evangelistic Ministries

The following organizations use a variety of opportunities—such as disaster relief, national missionary support, and child sponsorship—to bring the good news of salvation through Jesus Christ to people around the world. These ministries are ones our family has had personal experience with, and we recommend them to fellow Christians.

Billy Graham Evangelistic Association

Address: P.O. Box 779
            Minneapolis, MN 55440-0779
Phone: 877-2-GRAHAM (877-247-2426)
Web site: www.billygraham.org
E-mail: info@bgea.org

Ask for *Decision* magazine. This fruitful ministry has consistently used every communication venue available—television, print, radio, film—to deliver the gospel to every corner of the globe. Find out more from BGEA!

Campus Crusade for Christ

Address: 101 TDK Boulevard
              Suite B
              Peachtree City, GA 30269
Phone: 800-827-2788
Web site: www.campuscrusade.com
E-mail: CCCemail@campuscrusade.com

Campus Crusade provides tracts for evangelism, such as the "Four Spiritual Laws" booklet, and quality Christian books for discipling young people. Campus Crusade brings the good news of Christ's salvation to college campuses and communities across America and around the world. We are prayer partners with a Campus Crusade mission family (with three delightful kids) in Budapest, Hungary. They have had tremendous success bringing the gospel to Hungarian universities, public schools, and summer camps *and* training national workers!

Compassion International

Address: Colorado Springs, CO 80997
Phone: 800-336-7676
Web site: www.ci.org
E-mail: ciinfo@us.ci.org

Sign up for their E-mail lists. Through its child sponsorship program, Compassion presents the gospel to needy kids in over a dozen Third World nations along with education, skills training, medical attention, and food to "help release children from poverty, and enable them to become fulfilled Christian adults."

Gospel for Asia

Address: 1800 Golden Trail Court
Carrollton, TX 75010
Phone: 800-WIN-ASIA (800-946-2742); 972-300-7777
Web site: www.gfa.org
E-mail: info@gfa.org

Ask for *Send!* magazine and a free book by founder K. P. Yohannan. GFA supports more than 11,000 Asian missionaries who are reaching their own people for Christ in India, Thailand, Nepal, and 5 other Asian countries. GFA sponsors 45 missionary training centers with over 6,000 students, regular evangelistic outreaches, church planting, gospel films, and shortwave radio broadcasts in 13 Asian languages. GFA sends 100 percent of its donations to the field because all of the administrative staff at GFA's home office raise their own support, their building is paid off in full, and their vehicles have been donated. Christians can help sponsor a national missionary in India or another Asian nation for as little as $30.00 a month.

Jesus Film Project

Address: 910 Calle Negocio, Suite 300 (or P.O. Box 72007)
San Clemente, CA 92674-9207
Phone: 800-432-1997; 949-361-7575
Web site: www.jesusfilm.org
E-mail: jfp@ccci.org.

The *Jesus* film is a two-hour motion picture on the life of Jesus Christ filmed on location in Israel. The scenes were filmed on biblical sites where the actual events are believed to have taken place. All utility poles, antennae, and cars were removed for the shooting of the picture. All of the actors in the *Jesus* film are Israeli, except for Britain's Brian Deacon, who portrays Jesus. The dialogue in the script is taken directly from the book of Luke without embellishment or alterations. Filming took seven months.

To date, the *Jesus* film has been produced in 624 languages, including Afrikaans, Albanian, Arabic, Balinese, Thai, Tulu, Turkish, Turkmen, Ukranian, Urdu, Vietnamese, Welsh, Xhosa, Zarma, Zulu, and many others. A multi-stage translation process was used to dub each language to the film footage. Preliminary script approvals in each language were made by a committee of native-speaking persons. Language soundtracks were added to the film using frame-by-frame digital fitting. The *Jesus* Film Studio staff developed a digital lip-synchronization software to dub the voices in each language.

The *Jesus* film has been shown in 233 countries around the world. It has been shown on television stations in 167 nations. There are over 24.3 million copies of the *Jesus* video in circulation. By January 1, 2001, over 3.9 billion persons had seen the *Jesus* film. Invite some international college students or neighbors from another land to your home, and show them the *Jesus* video in their own language! Invite unsaved coworkers, neighbors, and friends over, and show them the English version.

Open Doors

Address: P.O. Box 27001
            Santa Ana, CA 92799
Phone: 949-752-6600

Web site: www.gospelcom.net/od/

Ask for *Newsbrief* newsletter. A set of fifty-two (one per week) pocket-size prayer cards for closed nations and persecuted believers around the world is available for $5.00. Open Doors supports Christians in countries around the world that are officially "closed" to missionaries and/or hostile to the gospel. Open Doors' "couriers" sneak much-needed foreign-language Bibles and songbooks into China, North Korea, the Middle East, etc. Through prayer and diplomacy, they support our Christian brothers and sisters who have been imprisoned or persecuted for their faith in Jesus.

Samaritan's Purse

Address: P.O. Box 3000
              Boone, NC 28607
Phone: 828-262-1980
Web site: www.samaritan.org
E-mail: info@samaritan.org

Ask for the E-mail ministry updates and monthly newsletter. Each Christmas Samaritan's Purse delivers donated shoe boxes filled with teddy bears, toys, toothbrushes, and Bible stories to hurting children around the world. Our kids love to help pack shoe boxes for others their own age and hear about the results. This Operation Christmas Child program has helped many kids in the Balkans, Ethiopia, Guatemala, and dozens of other nations come to know Jesus. Samaritan's Purse also enlists Christian medical personnel to help spread the gospel through its World Medical Mission outreach.

Voice of the Martyrs

Address: P.O. Box 443
Bartlesville, OK 74005
Phone: 800-747-0085; 918-337-8015
Web site: www.persecution.com
E-mail: thevoice@vom-usa.org

Ask for *The Voice of the Martyrs* magazine. Also available is a *Global Insight Prayer Calendar*, which focuses on a different restricted nation for prayer each month.

Other Resources
Multi-Language Media

Address: P.O. Box 301
Ephrata, PA 17522
Phone: (717) 738-0582
Web site: www.multilanguage.com
E-mail: mlminfo@multilanguage.com

Call or E-mail and ask for a copy of their excellent catalog, or view the catalog from their Web site.

Evangelical Council for Financial Accountability

Address: P.O. Box 17456
Washington, DC 20041-0456
Phone: 800-3BE-WISE (800-323-9473)
Web site: www.ecfa.org
E-mail: Webmaster@ecfa.org

ECFA's mission statement says, "ECFA is committed to helping Christ-centered organizations earn the public's trust through developing and maintaining standards of

accountability that convey God-honoring ethical practices."
Believers will be encouraged by the number of quality
ministries operating in our nation and around the world.
ECFA provides a list of many of them.

Visit ECFA's Web site at www.ecfa.org and click on
"Member Directory"; then use the "Search for" box to see
dozens of ministry categories, each with links to numerous
ministries. For example, "Mission-Foreign" lists over a
hundred organizations working worldwide to win people to
Christ. What a blessing!

Notes

Introduction

[1]This pledge is modeled after the "No-TV Week" contracts in Marie Winn, *Unplugging the Plug-In Drug* (New York: Penguin Books, 1987): pp. 174-175.

[2]Ibid., p. xiii.

[3]Ibid., pp. 56-7.

[4]Ibid., p. 146.

Chapter 1

[1]From John Wesley's (1739) translation of Paul Gerhardt's (1653) hymn, "Jesus, Thy Boundless Love to Me."

[2]"Do the Right Thing," *Bicycling* (November 1998): p. 69.

[3]Paul Bothrick, "5 Reasons Not to Leave the Country," *Discipleship Journal* (Issue 109): p. 94.

Chapter 2

[1]Michael Medved, "Saving Childhood," *Imprimis* (September 1998): p. 5.

[2]Robert Kubey is a member of the board of advisers of TV-Turnoff Network, which provided this information: www.tv-turnoff.org.

[3]Medved, p. 16.

[4]Winn, p. 211.

Chapter 3

[1]James B. Simpson, *Simpson's Contemporary Quotations* (Boston: Houghton Mifflin, 1988).

[2]For more information on the *Jesus* Film Project, see Appendix B.

[3]Scott Stossel, "The Man Who Counts the Killings," *Atlantic Monthly* (1997 May): p. 90.

[4]Ibid., p. 96.

[5]Ibid., p. 87.

[6]C. S. Lewis, *Mere Christianity* (New York: Touchstone Books, 1996): p. 93.

[7]James C. Dobson, *Dr. Dobson Answers Your Questions About Marriage and Sexuality* (Wheaton, IL: Living Books, 1982): pp. 86-88.

[8]Brian R. Clifford, *Television and children: program evaluation, comprehension, and impact* (Hillsdale, NJ: Lawrence Erlbaum Associates, Inc., 1995): p. vii.

[9]Winn, p. xiii.

[10]Joshua Meyrowitz, *No Sense of Place: The Impact of Electronic Media on Social Behavior* (New York: Oxford University Press, 1985).

[11]Joel Belz, "Why do we tolerate simulation when the real thing's not allowed?" *AFA Journal* (Nov/Dec 1997): p. 19.

Chapter 4

[1]These statistics come from two sources: Black, Bryant, and Thompson, *Introduction to Media Communication,* 5th ed. (Boston: McGraw-Hill, 1998): pp. 227-228 and "Facts and Figures," available from TV-Turnoff Network, http://www.tv-turnoff.org/FactsandfigPage.htm.

[2]Winn, p. 13.

[3]Victor C. Strasburger, *Adolescents and the Media: Medical and Psychological Impact* (Thousand Oaks, California: SAGE Publications, Inc., 1995): p. 12.

[4]Ibid., p. 12.

[5]Stossel, p. 92.

[6]Strasburger, p. 45.

[7]Jim Trelease, *The New Read-Aloud Handbook* (New York: Penguin Books, 1989): p. xv.

[8]Barna Research Group (1991). Available from http://www.barna.org.

Chapter 5

[1]Newton Minow, "The Vast Wasteland" in *The Annals of America, Vol. 18, 1961-1968: The Burdens of World Power* (Chicago: Encyclopedia Britannica, Inc., 1968): p. 14.

[2] Ibid., p. 15.

[3]Deirdre Donahue, "Is innocence evaporating in an open-door society?" *USA Today* (October 1, 1998): p. 2D.

[4]"How would you rate these programs?" *AFA Journal* (1998 May): p. 5.

[5]Rod Carveth, "Amy Fisher and the Ethics of "Headline" Docudramas," *Journal of Popular Film and Television* (v. 21, Fall 1993).

[6]Michael Medved, "Hollywood's Three Big Lies," *Reader's Digest* (October 1995): pp. 155-158.

Chapter 6

[1]S. Robert Lichter, et. al., *Watching America: What Television Tells Us about Our Lives* (New York: Prentice Hall, 1991): p. 27.

[2]Ibid., p. 28.

[3]Ibid., p. 29.

[4]Ibid., pp. 32-33, 36-37, 48.

[5]*USA Today* (1996 January 5): p. 1D.

[6]Keith Alexander, "'98 takes toll on media credibility," *USA Today* (December 16, 1998): p. 3B.

[7]Amy Mitchell, "The Big Picture: The Face of Local TV News Today," *Columbia Journalism Review* (January/February 1999): special report section with no page numbers.

[8]Ibid.

[9]Ibid.

[10]Tom Rosenstiel, Carl Gottlieb, and Lee Ann Brady, "Local TV News: What Works, What Flops, and Why" *Columbia Journalism Review* (January/February 1999): special report section with no page numbers.

[11]Tom White, "Human Rights or Rites of Passage?" *The Voice of the Martyrs* (April 1999): p. 4.

Chapter 7

[1]Winn, p. 139.